A Spiritual Journey to Allah
and His Messenger

Published by:

23-2 Jalan PJS 5/30, Petaling Jaya Commercial City
46150 Petaling Jaya, Selangor, Malaysia
+603-7772-3156 (office) / +6017-399-7411 (mobile)
info@tertib.press
www.tertib.press
@tertibpress (Facebook & Instagram)

Author	:	Abdullah Oduro
Transcriber & Editor	:	Najibah Nasruddin
Cover design	:	Abdul Adzim Md Daim
Book design	:	Abdul Adzim Md Daim
Printed by	:	Firdaus Press Sdn. Bhd.

MIGRATION OF THE HEART

First Edition: May 2021

Perpustakaan Negara Malaysia Cataloguing-in-Publication Data

Abdullah Oduro, 1980-
Migration of the Heart / Abdullah Oduro
ISBN 978-967-2420-80-4
1. Islam--Customs and practices.
2. Religious life--Islam.
3. Muslims--Conduct of life.
I. Title.
297.57

CONTENTS

INTRODUCTION

When I first became a Muslim, I read a book called *Ar-Risalat ut-Tabukiyyah*, or '*The Message from Tabuk*'. It was written by Ibn ul-Qayyim Al-Jawziyyah, may Allah have mercy on him, to a number of his pupils, companions and contemporaries as a reminder and an encouragement to seek knowledge. I do not intend to discuss the entire content of the book; however, I aim to highlight particular excerpts from it. When I read this book as a new Muslim, it allowed me to understand how to worship Allah correctly, glorified and exalted is He, the methodology of the Prophet, peace and blessings be upon him, and the companions that followed the Prophet in righteousness, as well as what it really means to get closer to Allah, glorified and exalted is He. In the process of reading, I remember not being able to put it down because it was very compelling. I told myself, "After telling my family about Islam, one day, I want to be able to relay the message of this book to somebody, *insha Allah*." Many years later, Allah, glorified and exalted is He, blessed me with the opportunity to worship Him by relaying some of the messages of this book that I found very inspiring to study Islam and to remain a Muslim.

I decide to come directly from Ibn Qayyim's statements. It is primary for us to understand the idea of his thought processes, from one general point to another, and we can observe this from the way he speaks and puts his words together, even in the English translation. Some have titled this book as *Zadul Muhajir Ila Rabbihi*, that is, the '*Provisions of the Traveller to His Lord*'. Thus, we are going to talk about issues that are primary to the said theme, particularly in dealing with the first pillar of Islam.

We call this discussion as the 'Migration of the Heart: The Spiritual Journey to Allah and His Messenger' because of the notion that we are travelling from one place to another. There is a beautiful story about a scholar named Fudhayl ibn Iyyad, may Allah be pleased with him. He was among the pious predecessors from around the time of Abdullah Mubarak, and he asked a beautiful question to a man that had come to him.

"How old are you?" asked Fudhayl ibn Iyyad. The man replied, "I am 60 years old." Fudhayl continued, "For sixty years, you have been on a journey to your Lord, and you are almost there." The man then replied, "*Innalilahi wa inna ilaihi rajiun.*" In any case, Fudhayl's response is a reminder to us all that this life is merely a journey. The response is profound because it reflected a response from one who ponders over life and thinks about death. When one ponders over life, he is thinking about the end of it. As a result, it encourages one to think about what he is going to do in his life. The reality of life itself is something that you are fully aware of.

The idea of this journey of life is also reflected in the numerous hadith of Prophet Muhammad, peace and blessings be upon him. One example was portrayed in a hadith when the Prophet took Ibn Umar, may Allah be pleased with him, by his shoulders and said, "Be in this world as though you are a stranger passing by." In this context, the meaning of 'stranger' is a wayfarer, or a traveller; in its Arabic term, a *Muhajir*, passing through a world that is temporary. In another example, Prophet Muhammad, peace and blessings be upon him, remarked, "What is the relationship between me and this world? Verily, I am like the traveller who sits under the shade of a tree, takes the shade of the tree, then gets up to continue his journey." This is a profound aspect when one learns about life through the lens of Islam; that this life is temporary. When we look at our age, we see that it is simply a journey to Allah, glorified and exalted is He, set at an appointed time that is unknown to us. The question we should ask ourselves is what are we doing to fulfil our primary principles and embody such principles in our lives?

THE HEART'S MIGRATION

Many may know the term '*hijrah*' as a form of migration from one place to another. In his book, Ibn Qayyim, may Allah have mercy on him, talks about two types of migration; the migration of the body, and the migration of the heart. Ibn Qayyim makes a certain point about these two migrations, that the physical migration that the body makes can only be the outcome of the heart's migration. We hear the word '*hijrah*' from the tale of the Prophet's migration, peace and blessings be upon him, from Makkah to Madinah. This was portrayed as a form of physical migration; however, the motivation behind it is the migration that we shall discuss as the second type of migration, the migration of the heart.

> "The behaviour of a migrator's heart requires migrating from one state to another."
>
> Ibn ul-Qayyim Al-Jawziyyah, *Ar-Risalat ut-Tabukiyyah*

The state that is mentioned by Ibn Qayyim, may Allah have mercy on him, in the above excerpt does not concern a physical location, rather a particular situation of the heart. In his book, Ibn Qayyim gives various examples of one's relationship with Allah, glorified and exalted is He; "Fear of other than Allah, to fear of Allah; love of Allah, to love of Allah." Through our discussion, we shall see the meaning of such manifestations, and how they connect to the first pillar of Islam, that is one's testimony of faith. Furthermore, Ibn Qayyim presents a verse in the Qur'an.

> "So, flee to Allah. Indeed, I am to you, from Him, a clear warner." *Adh-Dhariyat* (51:50)

In this verse, there is the Arabic word '*firru*', which means 'to flee'. In other words, a person is leaving something and going somewhere; the idea that there is a destination to arrive at. Moreover, the destination is a place where one finds safety and strength against the place that he is fleeing from. Therefore, whatever or whoever a person is fleeing from, the place that he is going to occupies the idea that it is stronger, or is able to protect him from a particular threat. In addition, this place may bring a sense of security, and other praiseworthy desires that he wishes.

> "Indeed, true *tawheed* requires fleeing from Allah, glorified and exalted is He, unto Him. Under the heading of 'from' and 'to'; therefore, falls a great reality of *tawheed*."
>
> Ibn ul-Qayyim al-Jawziyyah, *Ar-Risalat ut-Tabukiyyah*

In this statement, Ibn Qayyim presents the connection

of fleeing from one place to another with the great reality of *tawheed*. When a person flees from one place to another, there may be a possibility that there shall be a discrepancy, either in the process of the fleeing or the destination. If the hope behind fleeing is other than Allah, glorified and exalted is He, it is highly probable that would be a deficiency. However, in this example, Ibn Qayyim, may Allah have mercy on him, emphasises that should a person flee towards Allah, glorified and exalted is He, it is the manifestation and the great reality of *tawheed*.

> "O Allah, I seek refuge in Your pleasure from Your anger, and in Your forgiveness from Your punishment, and I seek refuge in you from you. I cannot reckon Your praise. You are as You have praised Yourself."
>
> Ibn ul-Qayyim Al-Jawziyyah, *Ar-Risalat ut-Tabukiyyah*

The Prophet, peace and blessings be upon him, recited this beautiful *du'a* during an episode with A'ishah bint Abu Bakr, may Allah be pleased with her. In the story, A'ishah was initially asleep in the night when she woke up to search for the Prophet, peace and blessings be upon him. When she found him, the Prophet was prostrating in his prayer. A'ishah, may Allah be pleased with her, reached out to touch the bottom of his feet when she heard the Prophet, peace and blessings be upon him, make this *du'a*. The *du'a* is profound because the Prophet was seeking refuge in Allah, glorified and exalted is He, from something that He owns as well. This is the ultimate manifestation of *tawheed*.

Whatever happens in this life occurs with the predestination of Allah, glorified and exalted is He. For example, the misguidance of the Prophet's uncle, Abu Talib ibn Abd al-Muttalib, had occurred because Allah allowed it to happen for an ultimate wisdom. In this instance, we observe the meaning of one of his 99 names, *Al-Hakeem*, being manifested. However, how does one react to such occurrences? Is the person seeking refuge in the protection of Allah, glorified and exalted is He, by making *dhikr*? Is the person seeking refuge by being patient with the predestination of Allah? If so, these are the manifestations of our *tawheed* that Ibn Qayyim highlights, may Allah have mercy on him.

> "There is neither fleeing from You, nor refuge but with You." Ibn ul-Qayyim Al-Jawziyyah, *Ar-Risalat ut-Tabukiyyah*

The above is another *du'a* that the Prophet, peace and blessings be upon him, had recited. When a person is fleeing from something that Allah, glorified and exalted is He, has predestined for him, that may also be detrimental to him, he is fleeing by doing and believing in things that please Allah. For example, from believing in a polytheistic practice that had been the lifelong tradition of his ancestors, the Prophet, peace and blessings be upon him, fled towards Allah, glorified and exalted is He; ultimately, trusting Him. Another example is the idea of infectious diseases. The COVID-19 virus is a disease that can harm a person. However, when a person flees towards Allah, he has firm belief and understanding that Allah, glorified and exalted is He, has ultimate control over everything, in addition to his patience towards Allah's predestination. Should a person fail to grasp this awareness, it could potentially lead to *shirk*, by believing that the creation of Allah, glorified and exalted is He, intrinsically has power over him. When a person believes and understands the circumstance that has occurred, and it is what Allah has carried out to test his patience and condition his strength, that is the manifestation of true *tawheed*.

In short, migration towards Allah, glorified and exalted is He, consists of abandoning what He dislikes, and doing what He loves and accepts. Migration then arises from a sense of love and hatred. Then, Ibn Qayyim, may Allah have mercy on him, brings forth a beautiful rule that is important for one to ponder over.

> "Obviously, a migrator, from one place to another, must have more love for the place to which he migrates than that from which he migrates, thereby giving preference to the location that is dearer to him."
>
> Ibn al-Qayyim al-Jawziyyah, *Ar-Risalat ut-Tabukiyyah*

Wherever the location a person is migrating to, he is going to have more love to get to that place, whether it is for protection from where he is leaving, or simply a desire for the place. Should his destination lead him to Allah, glorified and exalted is He, the ultimate motivation behind his action is migrating for the sake of Allah, trusting, believing, loving, fearing, being mindful of Him; all of which are different manifestations of *tawheed* and monotheism. Here, Ibn Qayyim presents the idea that a person's ultimate love of Allah, glorified and exalted is He, is granting him the drive to migrate towards a place that would bring him closer to his love.

Shaykh ul-Islam Ahmad ibn Taymiyyah, may Allah have mercy on him, the writer of *Al-Ubudiyyah*, or '*Servitude*', mentions a highly profound statement in his book. He elaborates on a particular hadith of the Prophet, peace and blessings be upon him. The content of the hadith is, "There are three things that should a Muslim find, then he has tasted the sweetness of faith." The first element of the three that is highlighted is that Allah, glorified and exalted is He, and His Messenger are the most beloved to him. The second element is that he does not love and care for another believer except for the sake of Allah. The third element is that he dislikes returning to disbelief, just as much as he dislikes returning to, or approaching, the Hellfire.

Shaykh Islam explains an intriguing point on the mentioned hadith.

> "This is a sign of complete love of Allah, glorified and exalted is He for verily, loving the beloved of your beloved is a sign of complete love for the beloved." Shaykh ul-Islam Ahmad ibn Taymiyyah, *Al-Ubudiyyah*

When a person loves something that is most beloved to the person, or thing, that he loves, that is the ultimate and complete love of the person, or thing, that you love. In other words, you love something simply because they love it. For instance, many of us may have grown up loving certain relatives because they have taught us everything we know. It could be our mother, father, brother, sister, or grandparents. Some scholars have mentioned that the main reason a person loves another is due to five factors; beauty, *ihsan*; the excellence of what he or she has done for us, the blessings of what he or she has given us, the qualities that he or she has that we hope for, and the relationship that we have with him or her. As a result, Allah, glorified and exalted is He, grants us these gifts; for some of us, He grants us all five gifts. Shaykh Islam mentions that these gifts are a symbol of the true love of Allah, glorified and exalted is He, that we love what He loves. When we observe our relatives, we will recognise the underlying reasons behind our love towards them would consist of the five factors. Our connection naturally strengthens because of how good they have been to us, the beautiful things they have done for us, and the hopes that we have of them and that such hopes have come through. We rely on them since we were children. When we reach the age of puberty, Allah, glorified and exalted is He, shifts the responsibility that He has initially placed on our parent or guardian onto us, that eventually we are held accountable for our own deeds. Allah, glorified and exalted is He, blesses us with this *fitrah* from His excellence and perfection. When we ponder over the love that we have for someone because of what he or she has done for us, and that the love strengthens the relationship, Allah, glorified and exalted is He, is a much greater example should we observe the countless of things that He has done for us. When we notice the things that He loves, and we love them because He loves them, that is a portrayal of love that is complete in perfection.

There is a beautiful *du'a* that was recited by the Prophet, peace and blessings be upon him, and it used to be a *du'a* that was recited by Prophet Dawud, peace be upon him. When the Prophet mentioned Dawud, peace be upon them, he would narrate about him by saying, "He was the best in worship out of all men." It should also be noted that there is weakness in the hadith.

> "O Allah, indeed, I ask You for Your love and the love of those who You love, and for the action that will cause me to attain Your love. O Allah, make Your love more beloved to me than myself, my family and cold water." *Tirmidhi*

It is interesting that cold water is mentioned in the supplication. During the time of the prophets, it was key to remember that many of them lived in warm climate countries, and that the weather was often very hot. In times of heat, cold water tends to be something that we take for granted when we have a lot of it. However, when we do not have water at all, it signifies a great challenge. That is the reason cold water is mentioned; it symbolises the reality of something that is very beloved to them, particularly during times of need. The Prophet, peace and blessings be upon him, recited this *du'a* to request from Allah, glorified and exalted is He, to make him of those that loves what He loves, and of the things that He loves, and to make the love a degree that is more beloved to Him than his own self.

> "A person *nafs*, desire, and devil keep inviting him to that which opposes what Allah loves and approves, and he is constantly tried by these things as they call him to what displeases his Lord. At the same time, the call of *iman* continues, directing him to what pleases his Lord; therefore, he should keep migrating to Allah at all times and should not abandon his *hijrah* until death." Ibn ul-Qayyim al-Jawziyyah, *Ar-Risalat ut-Tabukiyyah*

With regards to a person's *nafs*, desire, and the devil, the scholars have particularly spoken about the distinction between the *ruh*; the soul, and the *nafs*. The *ruh* and *nafs* are elements that leave the body when one dies. They are internal elements that make you, you. You are with your personality and characteristics. However, when these elements leave the body, all that is left is flesh. Ibn Qayyim also discusses this subject in his book entitled *Ruh*. He states, "Death is the departure of the soul from the body." When we die, our vision follows to move upwards as the soul leaves the body. The Prophet, peace and blessings be upon him, also noted on matter, "When the soul of a believer leaves the body, it is like a drip of water leaving from a faucet, smooth and easy. But, when the soul of a disbeliever leaves the body, it is like a prickly thorn leaving from a wet piece of wool."

Allah, glorified and exalted is He, mentions in the Qur'an about a group of people asking the Prophet, peace and blessings be upon him, about the *ruh*. This question also makes up the three questions that the scholars have mentioned as the introduction to the chapter of *Al-Kahf*, "They ask you about the *ruh* from the knowledge of Allah."

It is important to know that there are influences that will call us to oppose Allah. In the chapter *Al-A'raf*, verses 12 to 22, a dialogue between Allah, glorified and exalted is He, and *Shaytan* is presented. Here, it talks about the influence of *Shaytan* towards human beings. Between *Shaytan*, *Jinn*, and *Iblees*, there is a small difference. There is a *Jinn* that is good, and there is a *Jinn* that is bad. The *Shaytan* is slightly different. The *Iblees* is their father. Between these three creations of

Allah, all of them are set to call us to disobey Him, glorified and exalted is He. The battle between human beings and *Shaytan* is an ongoing battle until the end of time. In the said verses of chapter *Al-A'raf*, *Shaytan* says, "O Allah, leave me until the day they are resurrected." Allah, glorified and exalted is He, says, "Verily, I will leave you (to be of those with the mission that try to divert the people from the straight path)." Allah tells us to take *Shaytan* as our clear enemy. At the same time, the *nafs* also calls us to do evil as well.

> "It is amazing to find a man extensively and profoundly discussing the physical *hijrah* from the land of disbelief to the land of Islam, and the *hijrah* that ended with conquering Makkah though these forms of *hijrah* are incidental, and may never be required from him his entire life."
>
> Ibn ul-Qayyim Al-Jawziyyah, *Ar-Risalat ut-Tabukiyyah*

In the above excerpt, Ibn Qayyim, may Allah have mercy on him, continues to mention a state of *tarbiyyah*. It is not obligatory of us to perform migration. As the scholars have mentioned; it is sufficient for one to establish the five pillars of Islam. Ibn Qayyim also highlights that the physical migration may not be for everyone. However, the second type of migration; the migration of the heart, is obligatory upon everyone. Therefore, it is vital for us to understand the beauty of the heart's migration. Ibn Qayyim then poses the question, "Let us not get caught up with the physical idea of migration but rather, what was in their hearts that made them migrate?" When we observe what is said about the physical migration, it is not obligatory and is incidental. It is also the reason behind his statement about the wonder in finding man extensively and profoundly talking about the topic.

Here, we observe that the Prophet, peace and blessings be upon him, always took the opportunity to remind his companions about Allah, glorified and exalted is He. In a particular hadith, recorded during the Battle of Ta'if as some of the scholars have mentioned, the Prophet and his companions saw a woman with her child. The woman lifted her child and began breastfeeding. The Prophet, peace and blessings be upon him, asked his fellow companions, "Would you think that this woman would throw her child into a fire?" The companions responded, "No, Rasulullah, she would never throw her child into a fire." The Prophet then continued, "Allah is more kind to His slaves than this woman is to her child." We highlight this hadith because we find that the Prophet, peace and blessings be upon him, frequently took advantage of our senses, and tying the things that we observe or experience back to our *aqeedah*, or our belief. He, peace and blessings be upon him, did this as a method to remind us about the reality of Allah, glorified and exalted is He. As human beings, we tend to be more sensitive to the things that are present with us, or things that are in front of us.

This was portrayed through another example of hadith concerning of two camels. One camel was of a regular size, and the other camel was very skinny because it was sick. A Bedouin man was present with the Prophet, peace and blessings be upon him, and the two witnessed the two camels. The Bedouin man asked the Prophet a typical question, "Do we not see the two camels standing beside one another; therefore, one caused the other to fall sick?" The Prophet, peace and blessings be upon him, responded, "Yes; however, what caused the initial camel to fall sick?" The Prophet then went on to explain that there is no contagious disease that would infect a host without the permission of Allah, glorified and exalted is He, the Creator of the heavens and the earth. When we observe anything in life; even over the most mundane of occurrences such as the weather, we ought to remember the Creator behind them. Allah, glorified and exalted is He, asks us, "In your own selves, do you not see (the wonders)?" With the global pandemic, COVID-19, we learn that we have no control even over ourselves. Despite who we are, the role we hold, the amount of wealth we have;

we learn that we are merely weak against another creation of Allah, glorified and exalted is He. When one begins to reflect about life in and of itself, particularly during a time of ease, one can learn that that is a manifestation of the heart's migration.

> "But as for the *hijrah* of the heart, which is required from him as long as he breathes, you find that he does not seek any knowledge regarding it, nor does he develop any intention to undertake it. Thus, he turns away from that for which it has been created and which (*hijrah*) alone can save him, and involves him in that which of itself, cannot save him." Ibn ul-Qayyim Al-Jawziyyah, *Ar-Risalat ut-Tabukiyyah*

Ibn Qayyim, may Allah have mercy on him, continues to discuss about the idea of *tarbiyyah*. As we observe the verse of Allah, glorified and exalted is He, "I have not created *Jinn* nor mankind, except that they worship Me," we learn that the ultimate purpose of our creation is to show gratitude towards Allah. We also learn that this can be manifested in various ways throughout the *sunnah* of the Prophet, peace and blessings be upon him.

However, at times, a person may be tricked into performing a physical migration, particularly when he embarks and indulges upon a sound reason behind his migration. One may easily become over involved with the physical aspects of his migration, especially of those that he can see, and not the ultimate motivation, that is for the sake of *tawheed* and coming closer to Allah, glorified and exalted is He. Ibn Qayyim, may Allah have mercy on him, hones the kind of migration that builds a personal connection with Allah, glorified and exalted is He, one that constantly assists with turning back to Him during different aspects of our life.

> "And those who strive in our path, We will surely guide them to Our ways. And indeed, Allah is with the doers of good." *Al-Ankabut* (29:69)

The above is a beautiful and profound verse because it fulfils the two conditions for an action to be accepted. The verse observes three elements; the *nafs*, the desire, and the *Shaytan* who is constantly calling us to go against what Allah, glorified and exalted is He, wants us to do. For an action to be accepted, it requires two things; first, the intention is pure for Allah, glorified and exalted is He; second, the action is in accordance to what the Prophet, peace and blessings be upon him, has taught. For example, if a person claims there are, and prays, six obligatory prayers, the sixth prayer is rejected. His belief is also unaccepted because there are evidently only five prayers that are obligatory upon every Muslim.

The verse also highlights a result that is certain to demonstrate that Allah, glorified and exalted is He, will "surely guide them" to the straight path. Some scholars have mentioned that the 'path' refers to Paradise. Moreover, the noun '*muhsineen*' is used in the verse. The plural word of '*muhsineen*' comes from the singular word '*muhsin*'; it is derived from the word '*hasuna*', which means to beautify something. It presents an idea of excellence, but not perfection. This is the beautiful theme of Islam, that when a person aims to rectify his heart and actions, he does it to the best of his ability. For example, we are forced to face a number of trials during the pandemic, one of them being going into lockdown within our own homes. We spend more time with our families and consequently, some of our buttons may frequently be pressed. We would be tried with working online, or we would eventually grow tired of trying to adapt to the new circumstances. However, despite it all, we still persist to strive and struggle against the challenges. Allah, glorified and exalted is He, loves our struggle, and thanks us for that. As a result, the verse becomes meaningful because it reminds us to do our best; that the struggle is religiosity. Nobody can judge us except Allah, glorified and exalted is

He. Whether or not we will get to where we want to be as a result of our efforts may still be unknown; however, the fact that we care is a great blessing. Allah, glorified and exalted is He, answering the call is also a blessing.

The second portion is the migration to the Messenger of Allah, peace and blessings be upon him. This migration signifies a migration to Allah, glorified and exalted is He, and a symbol of *tawheed*. Scholars, including Ibn Qayyim, may Allah have mercy on them, have mentioned two categories concerning *ta'wheed*; first, knowing Allah's names and His attributes, glorified and exalted is He; second, knowing His lordship. When Allah speaks of His greatness, we come to learn and understand that He is in control of everything. With that knowledge of Allah, glorified and exalted is He, we ought to respond to that by calling Him. This is how we manifest the knowledge of Allah, and actualise it. This also represents the element of *tawheed uluhiyyah* within our worship, and the overall migration to Allah, glorified and exalted is He.

We should take into account the idea of conversion and reversion among us as Muslims. Some of us may be 'seasonal' Muslims; a term to describe that one only practices his religion and commit to his worship during particular periods. Others are yet to convert to Islam. Some may even be born as Muslims, and raised by Muslim families, but still find themselves 'converting' to Islam later in life. When we observe various Muslims of various ages and of various backgrounds, at times we recognise that a migration may not have necessarily taken place. A Muslim may testify his faith by reciting the *shahadah* and acknowledge his *tawheed*; however, what does it really mean to be a Muslim? Should a fellow Muslim be able to discover love towards his Lord should he dig deep inside his heart? Also, what does this love even mean? Such questions are vital to ask when a person has given his testimony of faith.

THE MIGRATION TO THE MESSENGER

> "The soul's journey in each of the issues of belief, and each of the heart's disposition, and in each of the affairs that arise and require ruling to the origin of guidance and source of light; coming from the mouth of the truthful and trustworthy (Muhammad, peace and blessings be upon him)." Ibn ul-Qayyim Al-Jawziyyah, *Ar-Risalat ut-Tabukiyyah*

The above excerpt is a definition of one's migration to the Messenger of Allah, peace and blessings be upon him, given by Ibn Qayyim, may Allah have mercy on him. Here, he highlights the journey, and the issues of belief. First, how do we believe in Allah, glorified and exalted is He? Does He have family ties? Is He a barbaric God? Does He make evil occur for the sake of evil? Or does He grant wisdom behind every occurrence? Is His wisdom better than our anticipation, and our anticipation of what we think should occur in life? When we ask ourselves these questions, it revises our initial creed, *'aqidah*, and belief in Allah, glorified and exalted is He. It also examines each of our heart's disposition towards Allah; in other words, our *fitrah*. '*Fitrah*' is the natural wiring that Allah, glorified and exalted is He, has created us with. It can also be observed as our 'end grain' characteristics. However, a person's *fitrah* has to be aligned and beautified, which brings us the subject of '*shariah*'. Allah, glorified and exalted is He, has brought forth the *shariah* to align the natural *fitrah* that all humans have, in order to beautify it. For instance, the *shariah* behind marriage. With Allah's will, all of us have a natural desire and are attracted to the opposite gender. However, in order to align and beautify this desire, one has to get married. It is a beautiful thing to love and to marry another, to have children, and to raise them upon the beautiful religion of Allah, glorified and exalted is He; overall fulfilling one's life purpose. Therefore, we should ask ourselves, in which direction are we looking towards when we observe the *halal* and *haram*? Where are we heading in the process of our life journey? When we are looking to buy a home, or carrying out our financial transactions, where should we go in order to attain truthfulness and beauty? In light of whose guidance am I looking towards? The answers to these questions are the lead to one's migration to the Messenger of Allah, peace and blessings be upon him.

The Prophet, peace and blessings be upon him, was truthful and trustworthy, which are two very important characteristics. In the documentation of the works of scholars, such as Ibn Qayyim himself, may Allah have mercy on him, we ought to try and empathise with people who spend their life reading the Qur'an, *sunnah*, and statements of scholars before them, to pour their heart out for the *ummah*. In the case of Ibn Qayyim, some of his works were documented in the midst of his travels. This was the *sunnah* of many scholars; when they speak or write, the contents of the Qur'an and *sunnah* were consistently running through their minds. As a result, this scholarship is produced through the words that they use, and the sequence of the words that they use. Therefore, when we study the works of Ibn Qayyim, we learn that the works have that type of presence.

> "Allah describes him as, 'Your companion (Muhammad) has not strayed, nor has he erred (2); Nor does he speak from (his own) inclination (3); It is not but a revelation revealed (4).'" *An-Najm* (53:2-4)

Ibn Qayyim, may Allah have mercy on him, brings this verse to remind us of what was mentioned earlier, "the mouth of the truthful and trustworthy." We ought to note that it was the practice of the scholars to ensure that there is proof behind their statements. In the verse given, the proof is the verse from chapter *An-Najm*, that Prophet Muhammad, peace and blessings be upon him, "does not speak of his own desires, of his own inclination," in which he was inspired. In various *seerah* documented, there may have been particular speech that had been delivered customarily; however, the Prophet, peace and blessings be upon him, never spoke of anything that Allah, glorified and exalted is He, would allow to lead people astray; to say of anything that would imply against the idea of monotheism, or of such nature.

Ibn Qayyim, may Allah have mercy on him, also notes an interesting statement that elaborates a type of misguidance that can be based on a lack of knowledge, and a type of misguidance that can be based on desires. He also calls attention to this subject in his other book, entitled *Risalah ila Ahadi Ikhwanihi*, also known as a letter documented for one of his brothers. Ibn Qayyim wrote, "With patience and certainty, one will reach leadership, authority, or empowerment in their religion." Here, 'patience' means when one is patient upon his desires. 'Certainty' means when one has knowledge, and is distant from misconceptions. The concepts of 'desire' and 'misconception' highlighted make up the notion of sin.

> "An issue is acceptable only if the light of his message irradiates it; otherwise, it deserves to be spunk into the sea of darkness."
>
> Ibn ul-Qayyim Al-Jawziyyah, *Ar-Risalat ut-Tabukiyyah*

Ibn Qayyim, may Allah have mercy on him, then brings the verse that confirms the prophethood of the Messenger, peace and blessings be upon him. The statement above is a very important principle. 'Principle' in Arabic is '*qa'idah*'. It comes from the word '*qa'ad*', and some of its definitions include 'to sit', 'stationary', something that 'does not move' or 'does not change'. This is the reason why principles are very important in our lives. When a person has a set of principles, he has a set of rules that he has established for himself that will not alter regardless of a change in place or time. Therefore, the light of the Prophet's message, peace and blessings be upon him, is a beautiful rule because it irradiates everything else. By using the lens of the *sunnah*, we validate and invalidate our actions and other occurrences that happen in our lives. Ibn Qayyim, may Allah have mercy on him, asks rhetorical questions that we should ponder upon regarding our actions, "Is this correct? Is this incorrect? Is this something that we should have our reservations with?" The way that he reminds us of the manifestation of our belief, and raises us with *akhlaq* through his writings is what makes Ibn Qayyim a *murabbi*.

"How, then, could a man who is enslaved by his base instincts and earthly inclinations undertake this migration? A man who does not want to

> part with the place where he was born and raised? A man who says, 'We only follow our father's way, hold to their tradition and trace their footsteps?' How could he undertake it when his ancestors were incapable of doing so and yet, he fully relies on them in determining his way of success and salvation, claiming that their opinions are better and sonder than his? If you investigate the reason for saying this, you find it is a combination of lingering on Earth, which is derived from laziness and indifference."
>
> Ibn ul-Qayyim Al-Jawziyyah, *Ar-Risalat ut-Tabukiyyah*

The incapability that is presented in the excerpt above shows that man is deficient, and Allah, glorified and exalted is He, owns the characteristics of perfection, making is impossible for Him to be incapable. Names such as *Al-Qawiy*, *Al-'Aziz*, *Al-Mateen*, *Al-Muhaimin*, and *Al-Jabbar*, that are taken from the 99 names of Allah, glorified and exalted is He, indicates this. Furthermore, Ibn Qayyim, may Allah have mercy on him, emphasises the act of blindly following our forefathers in terms of belief and practice. This is consistent with the contents of the Qur'an that are regarding tales of the Prophet, peace and blessings be upon him.

When the Prophet, peace and blessings be upon him, was presented with the revelation from Allah, glorified and exalted is He, the message was varied to that which his forefathers believed in and practiced. During the time of the Prophet, peace and blessings be upon him, the people, including his relatives, believed in polytheistic practices that were based on tradition. As a result, this portrayed their lack of struggle to seek for the truth; in turn, reflected the idea that Ibn Qayyim, may Allah have mercy on him, elaborated upon; laziness and indifference. It did not seem to occur to them to perform anything different than what was practiced at the time. It became clear that there were those who eventually came to recognise the preaching of the Prophet, peace and blessings be upon him, as teachings that were sound and intuitively right. However, many of them remained ignorant. This illustrates the way Ibn Qayyim, may Allah have mercy on him, notes on the reasoning behind the attitude of the people during the time of the Prophet, peace and blessings be upon him. Such insight comes from a kind of induction, that is reading from voluminous hadith, and being a scholar of the Qur'an. As learners, we ought to take this consideration when differentiating those who acquire scholarship, and those who lack thereof.

> "And similarly, We did not send before you any warner into a city except that its affluent said, 'Indeed, we found our fathers upon a religion, and we are, in their footsteps, following." *Az-Zukhruf* (43:23)

Ibn Qayyim, may Allah have mercy on him, continues by mentioning the above verse; a profound verse from the chapter *Az-Zukhruf* in his statement. The verse is so profound that there is a large portion in the book where the linguistic mechanism of the verse is further broken down to demonstrate the wisdom behind the verse.

> "But, no, by your Lord, they will not (truly) believe until they make you (O Muhammad) judge concerning that over which they dispute among themselves, and then find within themselves no discomfort from what you have judged, and submit in (full and willing) submission." *An-Nisa* (4:65)

Within the discussed context, Ibn Qayyim, may Allah have mercy on him, goes on to explain that the negation of *iman* is present until:

- The people make the Prophet, peace and blessings be upon him, their judge in all their affairs
- The people find no resistance with that that has been given to them from the *sunnah*
- The people are whole-heartedly compliant

Such points are also driven to highlight the psychological process that takes place within the fellow Muslim, in regards to the *sunnah*. Ibn Qayyim, may Allah have mercy on him, proceeds to mention:

> "This submission is not that of a defeated fighter who is forced to surrender to his enemy. Rather, it is the submission of an obedient subordinate to his master (Muhammad, peace and blessings be upon him) who is dearest to him, realising that only through this submission will he attain happiness and success."
>
> Ibn ul-Qayyim Al-Jawziyyah, *Ar-Risalat ut-Tabukiyyah*

Here, Ibn Qayyim, may Allah have mercy on him, highlights a person's submission to his Lord, aligning his words with the content of the verse of *An-Nisa* (4:65). He swears in the name of Allah, glorified and exalted is He, in Arabic, then the negation of *iman* is stated; although, at times, a negation is used before the actual swearing. Previously, we have discussed about the prophetic lens that we ought to envision our life through. When we come across disputes, which lens are we disputing through? When we wish to find a solution, what is the solution based upon, and where are we heading with the solution? Is our pathway consistent with our beliefs? The first step is to make the Prophet, peace and blessings be upon him, the judge behind our affairs, to which the Qur'an responds, "And they find themselves no discomfort." The second step is to be whole-heartedly compliant. Let us illustrate this situation through a story. It is a time of the pandemic. Due to the lockdown, you are sitting at home, unable to leave, unable to proceed with your plans, such as making hajj. You are unable to leave even for the mosque to make your routinely congregational prayers. You are generally frustrated at the overall circumstance, and as a result, there is a lot of negative energy within you. One day, you accidentally snapped at one of the members within the household. A dispute occurs, and one of you seek the advice of someone who is more knowledgeable, respected for their wisdom and religion, and preferably unbiased towards the dispute. Suddenly, the one person that you had hoped could give a neutral view and advice, favours with the one that you disputed with. In that situation, would you find a level of contentment? Ibn Qayyim, may Allah have mercy on him, questions in his book, "How many people protest and say, 'I wish this particular *sunnah* was not mentioned,' or 'I wish the Prophet, peace and blessings be upon him, would not have said that.'"

Each and every one of us may have experienced a time where we were carrying out a certain action, and with the *qadr* of Allah, glorified and exalted is He, another person may have advised us against the action due to its wrongness. Then, we come to learn, "The action that I was doing is prohibited in Islam? But I have been doing this for so many years." Particularly for those who have just started to consistently practice their faith, we may feel a tightness in our hearts due to this discovery. However, Allah, glorified and exalted is He, informs us that it is a process for one to endure. Those who comply and follow the *sunnah*, the Qur'an states, "They do not find within themselves any discomfort." For those who possess true *iman* and are in total submission, they do not find any hardship. An Arabic saying notes, "Those that know, know. Those that do not know, do not." The people who practice the *sunnah* of the Prophet, peace and blessings be upon him, are aware of the sweetness of faith that comes with their actions, and experience true happiness. For those who are still in the process of learning to reach such a state, we ought to ask ourselves, "What is the effort that we are making to achieve this?"

Regarding the *sunnah*, more often than not, many of us tend to feel that we are forced to perform them, particularly when it involves a *sunnah* that we are very discouraged to do, whatever it may be. I recall a story of a brother of mine who complained about his son not wanting to perform his *Fajr* prayer. He was trying to wake his son, when the son responded, "I don't want to do this anyway." The son preferred sleep over making his prayer. The wisdom behind this story is that it is beyond our capabilities to force anyone to do what is right by Allah, glorified and exalted is He. Furthermore, there are also instances when we carry out certain actions as Muslims along with other Muslims, without any honest intention, and simply to be a part of the group. We may tell ourselves, "I want to look religious. It's a cool thing to do." Without a doubt, it is always good to want to be around good people, and to be influenced with goodness. However, there shall come a time when you have to learn and understand the wisdom behind such actions. Did the Prophet, peace and blessings be upon him, perform these actions? When we learn about the greatness of Allah, and the process of selecting the greatest human being there is for prophethood, we shall learn that all of it leads back to one who defines the very idea of greatness itself; Allah, glorified and exalted is He. However, the master that is referred to in the said verse of the Qur'an is Prophet Muhammad, peace and blessings be upon him — why? Because the verse that was stated in chapter *An-Najm*, that the Prophet never speaks with his own desires. The wisdom behind establishing a set of rules to live by is that we shall always have something to refer to whenever we experience unease. Taking the story of our brother who was struggling to wake his son for *Fajr* prayer as our example; why do we have to wake up for prayer? Allah, glorified and exalted is He, is *Al-'Aleem*, the one who sent the Prophet, peace and blessings be upon him, to tell us about the prayer. Therefore, we ought to place our trust in Him. This is the process of how one may strengthen his love for the Prophet with a continuous struggle. Ibn Qayyim, may Allah have mercy on him, informs us of this process through the verses of the Qur'an that become the foundation of our connection to the Creator.

THE CALL FOR SELF-REFLECTION

> "If a person wishes to know where he stands in regards to this matter, he should examine himself, and inspect his heart when a judgement from the Messenger, regarding a major or minor issue, comes conflicting with his desire, or differing from the way of his ancestors…"
>
> Ibn ul-Qayyim Al-Jawziyyah, *Ar-Risalat ut-Tabukiyyah*

Referring to the excerpt above, Ibn Qayyim, may Allah have mercy on him, brings forth the academic portion of the discussion. He questions, "How do we self-reflect? How do we hold ourselves accountable in regards to the *sunnah*?" He continues by presenting the verse of Allah, glorified and exalted is He, in chapter *Al-Qiyamah* as his response.

> "Allah says: Rather, man, against himself, will be a witness (14), Even if he presents his excuses (15)." *Al-Qiyamah* (75:14-15)

We know ourselves best. We know our desires, and denying the things that are more beneficial to us. However, despite us knowing so, there are times when we give ourselves excuses to fall into our desires, and that is the plan of *Shaytan*. Nevertheless, there has to be a limit to this, where we stand up to ourselves and say, "Let me do what is best for me, because I know that it is better for me." In the verse above, Allah, glorified and exalted is He, tells us that we hold ourselves accountable. Umar ibn Al-Khattab, may Allah be pleased with him, had once stated, "Hold yourself accountable before you will be held accountable." In other words, he implores us to weigh our own deeds before they will be weighed. One way for us to do this is to observe the actions we have carried out in a day. Before we go to sleep, ask Allah, glorified and exalted is He, to forgive us should we have done anything wrong, or thank Allah should we have done something right.

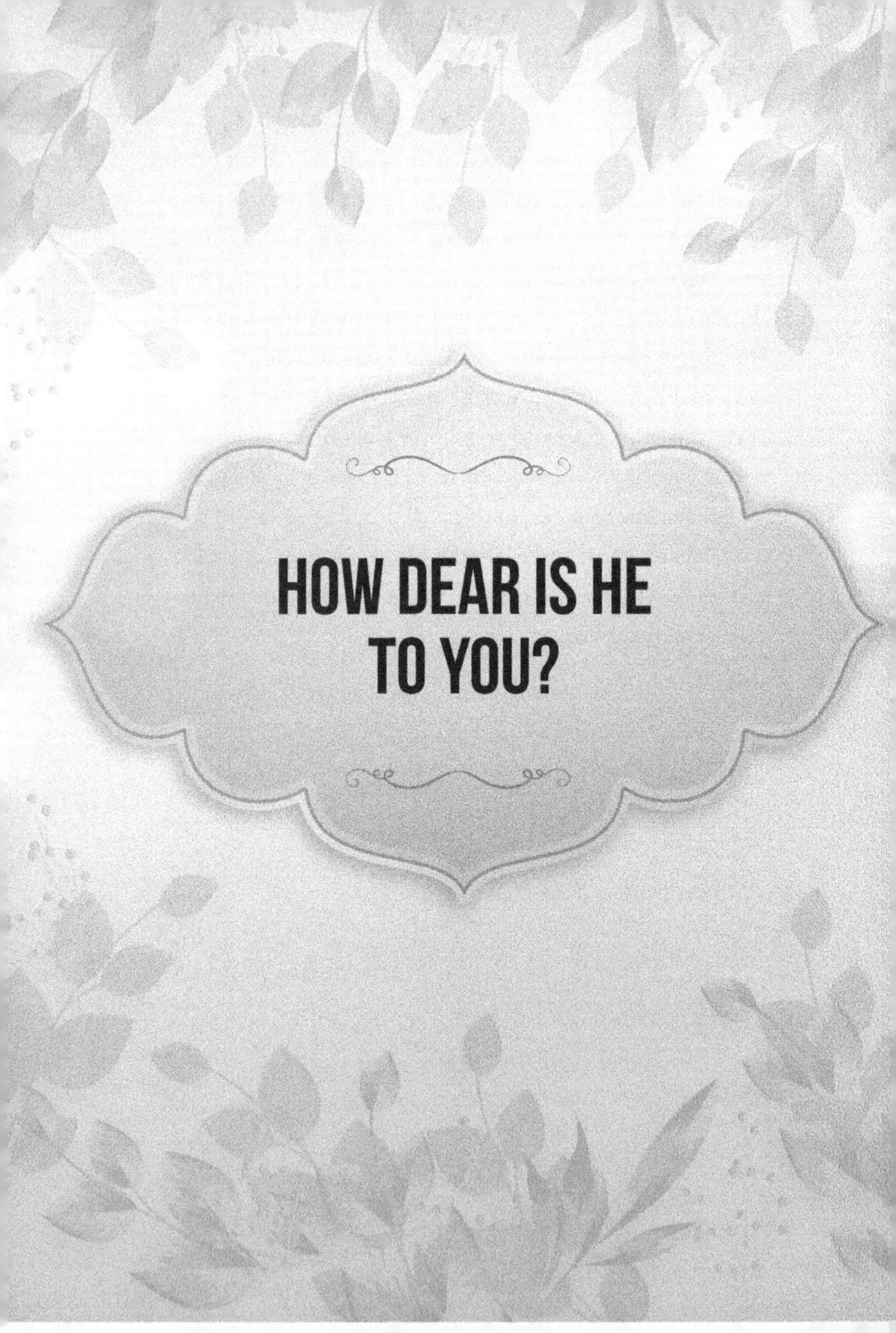

HOW DEAR IS HE
TO YOU?

How dear is the Prophet, peace and blessings be upon him, to you? Ibn Qayyim, may Allah have mercy on him, mentions two ways to understand how dear the Prophet is to us.

> "Allah says, 'The Prophet has a higher claim on the believers than they have on themselves.' This verse indicates that anyone who does not give more regard to the Messenger than oneself is not one of the believers." Ibn ul-Qayyim Al-Jawziyyah, *Ar-Risalat ut-Tabukiyyah*

The verse above presents the first way for one to understand how dear the Prophet, peace and blessings be upon him, is to us. Particularly referring to individualism, one ought to ask, "How can I love someone more than I love myself?" When I was in high school, we had to watch the film *Romeo & Juliet*. The film taught me that a person would be willing to die in the place of another should he or she love the person more than him or herself. With regards to the Prophet, peace and blessings be upon him, he is unlike any other human being. There is none other like him, and there shall be no other like him. This is because he has been given the revelation by Allah, glorified and exalted is He, which changes his status among other human beings. However, it is not him who we worship. We ought to love the Prophet, peace and blessings be upon him, more than we love ourselves because of the three elements that we touched upon earlier in the discussion; our *nafs*, desires, and the devil that can influence us. By following the teachings of the Prophet, peace and blessings be upon him, Allah would not allow us to be misguided by those elements because of the fact that He, glorified and exalted is He, has chosen Muhammad, peace and blessings be upon him, as His Messenger. We know this by referring to the verse *An-Najm*; "He (Muhammad) does speak with his own desires." When the Prophet speaks, he is inspired by the divine revelation. His speech is not from a place that would misguide mankind because of the fact that he has a lifelong mission. This distinction is important for us to understand. For all these reasons, we ought to love the Prophet, peace and blessings be upon him, more than we love ourselves because Allah, glorified and exalted is He, is using him as a medium to profess the His divine message.

> "Recognising the Prophet's claim over one's self, and loving him truly results in all of the true consequences of love..." Ibn ul-Qayyim Al-Jawziyyah, *Ar-Risalat ut-Tabukiyyah*

As mentioned previously, the first requirement is that

the Prophet, peace and blessings be upon him, should be dear to oneself more than one's own self. Ibn Qayyim, may Allah have mercy on him, then continues:

> "Indeed, there is a great difference between knowing the meaning of love, and being truly in love. People often confuse knowledge and experience." Ibn ul-Qayyim Al-Jawziyyah,
>
> *Ar-Risalat ut-Tabukiyyah*

Referring to the excerpt above, many of us may know the difference between the meaning of love, and being truly in love on a psychological level. It is very important for us to be able to make this distinction. Ibn Qayyim, may Allah have mercy on him, questions, "You may be infatuated with something, but are you truly in love with it?" There is a vast difference between the two areas, and it also signifies the final frontier for many fellow Muslims. Those who observe Muslims and the actions that they carry outwardly as Muslims may say, "I love the fact that you pray five times a day," or "I love the fact that you worship one God," or "I love the fact that Prophet Muhammad was a person of righteousness, and was extraordinarily kind to others, and exhibited the epitome of manhood." The Prophet, peace and blessings be upon him, was an exceptional reformer.

However, as Muslims, we must always remember that he is a prophet of Allah first. This is because any individual who is not a prophet, can be a reformer. However, a prophet chosen by Allah, glorified and exalted is He, is a figure of an incomparable level. Ibn Qayyim, may Allah have mercy on him, notes on this difference and urges us to ponder, "Are we infatuated with the idea of loving the Messenger, or do we truly and sincerely love the Messenger?" Shaykh ul-Islam Ahmad ibn Taymiyyah, a respected scholar in the field, had once described the idea of true love towards your beloved as 'loving what your beloved loves'. When a person loves something simply because the Prophet had loved it, then he has attained the true love of the Messenger, peace and blessings be upon him. From time to time, we ought to stop and ask ourselves, "Do I have a dislike in my heart towards the *sunnah* of the Prophet, peace and blessings be upon him?" This is what Ibn Qayyim, may Allah have mercy on him, encourages us to think about, that people "often confuse knowledge with experience."

For those who are familiar with *Yaqeen Institute*, I work with the Convert Life department there, and there is a beautiful paper that I would advise you to read, that has been written under the institute. The paper was written by a good friend of mine, and is entitled '*Souls Assorted*', which discusses about spiritual personalities. The paper makes the distinction of the way some people learn with experience, and others learn with knowledge. Regardless, one should not be neglected of the other; the two should rather be combined. For example, people who naturally learn through experiences are more prone to certain things, yet one should not defy the other. A person ought to have the benefit of both methods, and Ibn Qayyim, may Allah have mercy on him, makes a beautiful distinction in relation to this.

> "A person who claims that the guidance is not to be sought from him, but from the dictates of the mind, and who claims that the Messenger's message does not offer certitude?" Ibn ul-Qayyim Al-Jawziyyah, *Ar-Risalat ut-Tabukiyyah*

Here, Ibn Qayyim, may Allah have mercy on him, asks a rhetorical question, and many of us may fall into this way of thinking. In my experience, I had come across a brother who had converted to Islam, who asked the purpose behind using *miswak* to clean one's mouth. He asked, "Why do we have to use a *miswak*? We can use a normal toothbrush, now that toothbrushes are invented," implying the idea of outdatedness with regards to the *miswak*. In this situation, I was driven to ask myself, "Even if we do use the *miswak* instead of a toothbrush, does it signify a lack of intellect?

Is it backwards, or is it the *sunnah* of the Prophet, peace and blessings be upon him, and is timeless? This is where scholarship comes in. Nevertheless, if a person understood the idea of performing the action of his beloved because of his love towards him, and the Prophet cleaned his mouth using the *miswak*, the person would solely clean his mouth using the *miswak* simply because the Prophet, peace and blessings be upon him, did so. This is the love of the Messenger that is elaborated about, that we ought to want to do it because he did it. Should we observe a *sunnah*, and we respond with uncertainty, "Well…I don't know if I want to do it…" That kind of response would display a conditional type of love. When we discuss about the love of the Prophet, peace and blessings be upon him, it should not be conditional because it has been granted by Allah, glorified and exalted is He. Moreover, as we have highlighted previously, what should be the yardstick of determining the right and wrong within our lives? We learn that Allah has given human beings the *'aqal* to think and decide. However, the scholars of *usul fiqh* have mentioned that using the *'aqal* alone to determine the right and wrong is not enough, and may even lead one to destruction. To think and decide requires a combination of the *'aqal*, and the *sunnah* of the Prophet, peace and blessings be upon him. One should note that the *'aqal* should also be from a place of sound intellect, which also falls into accordance of the *sunnah*.

> "These, and other similar views reflect deviation from the Prophet and his message, and substitution of the beneficial knowledge by what is inferior to it. This indeed is clear misguidance." Ibn ul-Qayyim Al-Jawziyyah, *Ar-Risalat ut-Tabukiyyah*

When a person uses his intellect as an independent source of guidance, or even an independent source of determining what he wants to take from the *sunnah*, it creates a pathway to misguidance. We have discussed about the idea of making the Prophet, peace and blessings be upon him, one who is most dear to us, and that he should be the ruler over us. In the excerpt above, Ibn Qayyim, may Allah have mercy on him, explains a situation when a person decides to be a ruler of himself, for himself. This exemplifies a type of deviation from making the Prophet, peace and blessings be upon him, the ruler over our lives.

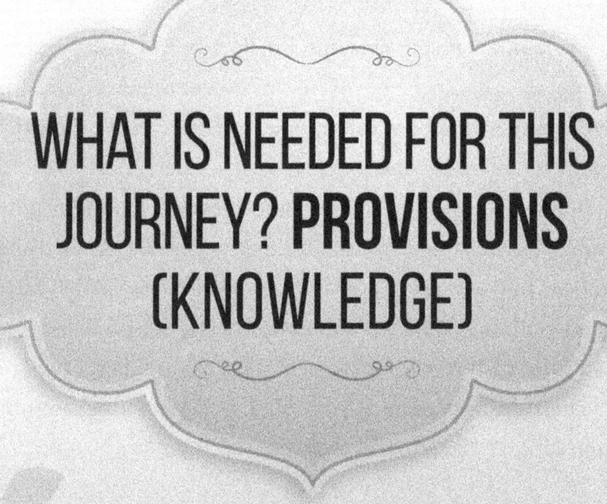

WHAT IS NEEDED FOR THIS JOURNEY? **PROVISIONS** (KNOWLEDGE)

In the earlier portions of our discussion, we have highlighted what it means to follow, or to be on a journey towards the Prophet, peace and blessings be upon him. Later on, we explained the way a person makes the Prophet dear to himself, and the signs that symbolise this endearment. We covered one verse from the chapter *An-Nisa* (65:4) that demonstrates a milestone for determining a person's obedience, allegiance, and love towards the Prophet, peace and blessings be upon him. The journey that we have discussed about is still a journey that we are all on. The first requirement that Ibn Qayyim, may Allah have mercy on him, mentions is provisions; in other words, knowledge. Therefore, the first thing that we need to have on our journey is knowledge.

> "The provisions for this journey are the knowledge inherited from the seal of the prophets — there are no other provisions. Is it enough to get you to your destination? The danger of lagging behind on this journey, and being with those who lag behind on this journey, and being with those who lag behind voluntarily. 'And never will it benefit you on that Day, when you have wronged, that you are (all)

sharing in the punishment.'" *Az-Zukhruf* (43:39), Ibn ul-Qayyim Al-Jawziyyah, *Ar-Risalat ut-Tabukiyyah*

Ibn Qayyim, may Allah have mercy on him, continues to mention the lines of Al-Khansa's poem, a pious lady of the past. The poem was written because one of her brothers had passed away. Ibn Qayyim makes a very profound distinction.

> "If it were not for the numerous people wailing around me over their brothers — I would have killed myself. And none of them wails over the likes of my brother. Yet, I comfort myself in that we all share (the misery)." *Al-Khansa*

In this poem, Al-Khansa tells the tale that other people were wailing over their deceased relatives, which had brought some comfort to the passing of her own brother because she was not alone in her grief. In relation to the verse of chapter *Az-Zukhruf* taken from the excerpt of Ibn Qayyim's book, he presents this poem with the intention to illustrate that sharing a punishment will neither bring us comfort nor benefit on the Day of Judgement. In this life, we may find comfort when we see other people sharing a cry, or the same state of sorrow as us. We would share feelings of sympathy and empathy. However, should we become individuals who decide to depart from the journey to the Messenger, or depart from following the *sunnah* of the Messenger, peace and blessings be upon him, we shall end up on the pathway to ignorance. Some scholars mention that there are two types of ignorance; based on *usul fiqh*, there is a minor ignorance, and a compound ignorance. In addition to that, there is also the ignorance of not knowing something, and the ignorance of knowing, yet not acting upon it. As Muslims committed to seeking knowledge for the provisions of our journey, these are the different categories of ignorance that we ought to protect ourselves from.

THE WAY (ACTION)

"The way for accompanying this journey is by exerting full capacity, and striving to the extreme. It cannot be accomplished by wishing, nor obtained through loitering." Ibn ul-Qayyim Al-Jawziyyah, *Ar-Risalat ut-Tabukiyyah*

The second requirement that is needed for the journey to the Messenger, peace and blessings be upon him, is a pathway; in other words, an action. In order to reach the desired destination, a person has to act and move. Some of us may have the knowledge, but have yet to act upon that knowledge. If we have the knowledge, but do not act upon it, the knowledge may be something that goes against you on the Day of Judgement. It portrays a sense of responsibility towards the acquired knowledge, in comparison to taking advantage of it. Moreover, it shows our sense of humility that we have towards Allah and His Messenger; that we should not be concerned over the thoughts of other people in the process of our journey, and that we should persist regardless of the response that we may receive from it, because we know it is the right thing to do, even if we are estranged.

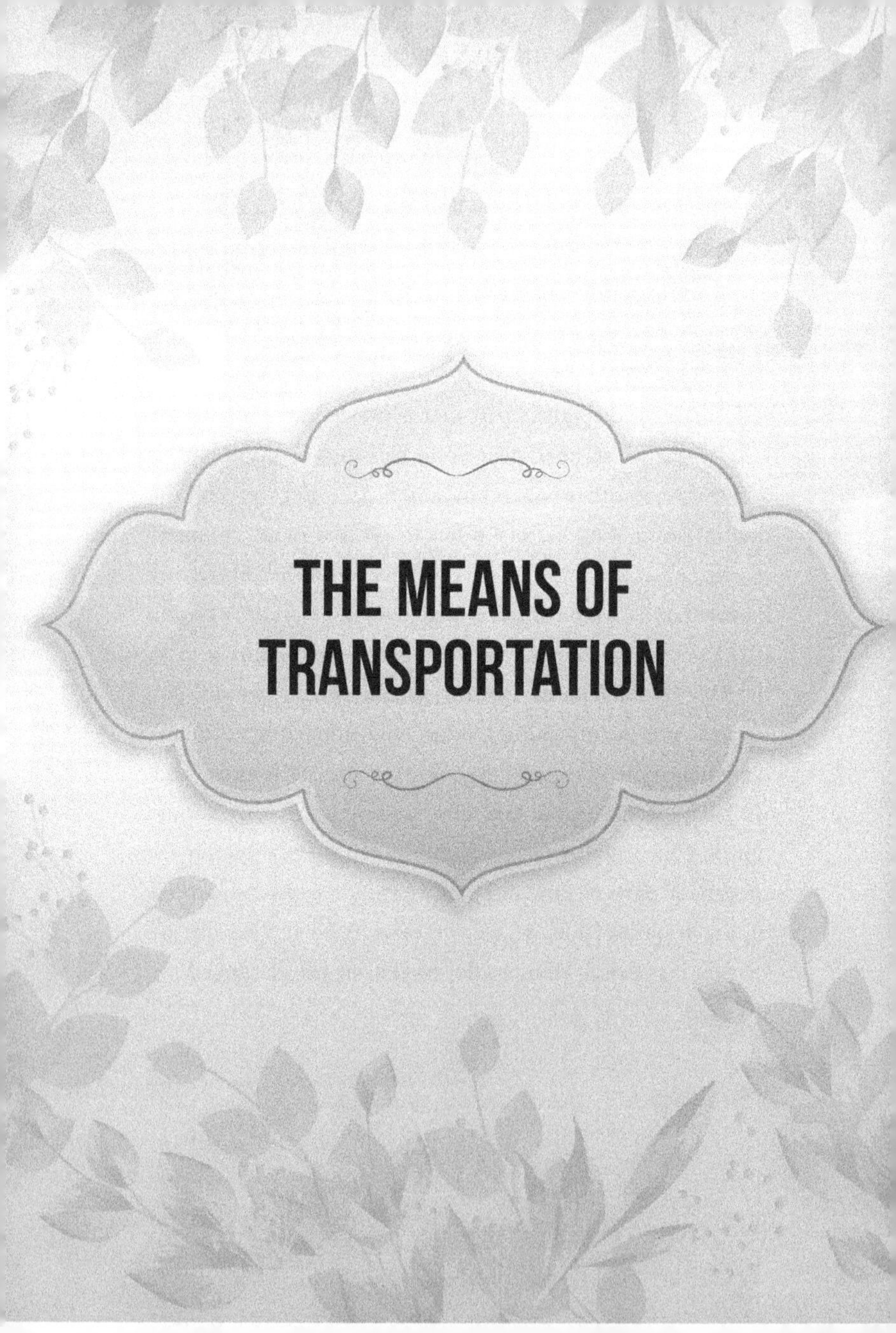

THE MEANS OF TRANSPORTATION

The third requirement that is needed for the journey to the Messenger, peace and blessings be upon him, is our means of transportation. How are we going to get there? Ibn Qayyim, may Allah have mercy on him, says that the vehicle of transportation in the journey of one's migration is:

- Truthfully taking shelter in Allah
- Turning to Allah whole-heartedly
- Imploring Allah sincerely
- Exhibiting absolute reliance in Allah
- Putting full confidence in Allah
- Falling before Allah like a subdued and defeated person who possesses nothing — a person who looks up to his master for dignity and security, and for obtaining some of His bounties, hoping that He would shelter him.

  Ibn ul-Qayyim Al-Jawziyyah, *Ar-Risalat ut-Tabukiyyah*

All of these points are the manifestations of *tawheed*. Truthfully taking shelter in Allah, glorified and exalted is He, is trusting in His name; *Al-Hafidz*, or trusting His greatness; *Al-'Aziz*, or having *tawakkul*; to truly seek shelter from Him and not from anything else. Turning to Allah, glorified and exalted is He, is to turn to Allah even after making a mistake. Imploring Allah, glorified and exalted is He, sincerely is to call upon Him, and not upon anyone or anything else; to call upon Him firstly, initially or only. Exhibiting absolute reliance on Allah, glorified and exalted is He, is having sincere *tawakkul* in Him by asking ourselves, "Do we lay all of our confidence in Him?" Many of us may believe in Allah. We believe that He is the one, true God, He was not born, He does not pro-create, and there is nothing that is like Him. However, do we believe Allah? When we lose our job or our family members, or when we experience divorce, or when we are unable to bear children, where do we mentally and spiritually turn to? Moving on to the following point; the epitome of servitude. This is where we fall before Allah, glorified and exalted is He, like a subdued and defeated person, knowing that Allah has ultimate control, and we have and are nothing without Him. These are the mentality, methodology, and spiritual connection that one should have when he is on his journey; he travels in these said manners. This is the vehicle that is being described.

COMPANIONS ALONG THE WAY

By now, Ibn Qayyim, may Allah have mercy on him, have mentioned the notions of following Allah, glorified and exalted is He, and following the Messenger, peace and blessings be upon him. As a result, he has covered the first pillar of Islam, that, "There is no God but Allah, and the Prophet Muhammad is His Messenger." This illustrates the final migration to Allah and His Messenger; at the very end, Ibn Qayyim mentions such provisions. For example, there are occasions where you read the books of scholars, and they highlight a matter that you may ponder upon, "But how do I do this?" Within the next line, the book answers the question. In this situation, Ibn Qayyim, may Allah have mercy on him, has given us the foundation of Islam. Through his writings, he raised us, taught us the manners, and exemplified principles. Later, presents to us the tools we would need in order to carry out this quest correctly. The companions along the way refer to the people we should have with us on our journey. The first that Ibn Qayyim notes is to 'live with the dead'.

> "He who intends to undertake this journey should accompany the dead who are, in reality, alive. Their company will enable him to reach his goal. He should avoid the company of the living who are, in reality, dead — they will only

disrupt his course." Ibn ul-Qayyim Al-Jawziyyah, *Ar-Risalat ut-Tabukiyyah*

From the first portion of the statement, Ibn Qayyim, may Allah have mercy on him, advises us to follow those who have passed on from this world. Among them are the companions of the Prophet, peace and blessings be upon him, and fellow scholars, including Ibn Qayyim himself. This is the group of people who we ought to follow and busy ourselves with. We ought to take their company, study about their lives, and read their works and what they have to say. As we discuss the contents of the present book, we are reading and studying the message of Ibn Qayyim, may Allah have mercy on him, who is teaching us the foundation of Islam via a migration to Allah, glorified and exalted is He, and His Messenger, peace and blessings be upon Him.

"Indeed, it is We who bring the dead to life, and record what they have put forth, and what they have left behind, and all things We have enumerated in a clear register." *Yasin* (36:12)

Once again, Ibn Qayyim, may Allah have mercy on him, brings a verse from the Qur'an to substantiate statement, presenting proof for a very important aspect of Islam, that is scholars and their scholarship. The above verse is also the very reason why he advises us to "live with the dead", to demonstrate that the dead presents a strong message that lives on. In every gathering and at every mosque that he has attended or taught, there is not one that Ibn Qayyim does not mention and have *Riyad as-Salihin* by Imam Nawawi. Therefore, his message, *fiqh*, and his understanding of Islam lives on within all of us. This is the idea that Ibn Qayyim, may Allah have mercy on him, calls attention for, to spend our time with the dead, and avoid wasting time with matters that are dead to the heart. The Prophet, peace and blessings be upon him, said, "The one who remembers Allah in comparison to the one who does not is like a house that is empty," meaning that there is no life within it. Allah, glorified and exalted is He, mentions to follow the message, "If he calls you to that which livens you," referring to matters that bring us life. Scholars, including Ibn Qayyim, often remind us that, "Allah is the one Who gives us life." Thus, we should busy ourselves with the remembrance of Allah, glorified and exalted is He, the very least, during some parts of our week, and strive to do so on a daily basis because that is best for us.

"The scholars will be here until the end of time." Ali ibn Abi Talib

In an advice that he had shared with a person, Ali ibn Abi Talib, may Allah be pleased with him, shared the above statement. He had also mentioned, "You cannot see them, but their examples are present in our hearts."

> "Whoever wishes to tread a path (methodology), let him or her tread the path of those who have passed away." Ibn Mas'ud

In the same context, Ibn Mas'ud also mentioned the beautiful statement above. At times, it may be difficult for us to protect ourselves from the drama, or *fitnah*, that follow with those who are alive. For instance, the dynamics of social media, and the attitude and behaviour of the community that follows with online interactions. My personal advice to myself and my friends is prevent busying oneself with the comments that we may receive regarding our posts and shares online. By reading the comments, a person risks his reaction and response, particularly when it is a tabloid issue. Some of the ways that we can tackle this is by changing the page, or going to a different section. Most importantly, we ought to reduce busying ourselves with social media, unless it concerns matters that remind you of Allah, glorified and exalted is He. If the activity that we engage with online does not remind us to be a person of honour, dignity, integrity, and positivity, we should avoid wasting our time with it altogether. Our time is limited, and we must remember that we are on an ongoing journey.

> "You must then avoid the company of the ignorant associates, seeing instead the company of those who are absent in person, but whose bounties and good influence continue to exist in the world." Ibn ul-Qayyim Al-Jawziyyah, *Ar-Risalat ut-Tabukiyyah*

Based on the above statement, Ibn Qayyim, may Allah have mercy on him, encourages us to avoid the company of ignorant people; however, seek to be in the company of those who are absent in person; in other words, in the presence of those whose influence lives on.

THE HUMBLE STRANGER

The last portion of the discussion is about a humble stranger. Ibn Qayyim, may Allah have mercy on him, proceeds by giving a beautiful advice.

> "When you do the above, you will acquire a new zeal and direction, and will become a stranger among people — even if you are known or related to them. You will be a distinguished stranger among them; clearly seeing the obscurity they suffer, though they cannot see the splendour you enjoy."
>
> Ibn ul-Qayyim Al-Jawziyyah, *Ar-Risalat ut-Tabukiyyah*

For some of us, we may be the only member who practice Islam within the family. For example, we may be trying to pray five times a day consistently, while our other family members are not. As a result, our actions may be commented upon due to the fact that we are different from the rest of the members. Ibn Qayyim, may Allah have mercy on him, alludes us with the fact that we may be the only one attempting to follow the path of the Prophet, peace and blessings be upon him.

"Look at them with two eyes:

1. One eye recognises Allah's commandments and

prohibitions, leading you to advise and warn them, befriend or disown them, giving them their rights and acquiring yours.

2. The other eye recognises Allah's decree and measure, leading you to sympathise with them, supplicate and seek forgiveness for them, and seek excuses for them in matters that do not involve violation of Allah's commandments and *shariah.* Thus, you engulf them with kindness, compassion, and forgiveness, heeding Allah's commandment to His Messenger."

Ibn ul-Qayyim Al-Jawziyyah, *Ar-Risalat ut-Tabukiyyah*

The first eye refers to the eye that understands the principles that Allah, glorified and exalted is He, has ordered and prohibited, and we call the good and forbid the evil based on this eye. The second eye refers to the decree and measure of Allah. This means understanding the situation the people are in; with Allah's commandments and prohibitions, we ought to look at those who are not performing their prayers, being dishonest, being negative, or who are really tested, and try to advise them to the best of our abilities. We may even have to leave several people in our lives because of their negative effect on you. In a tale of the Prophet, peace and blessings be upon him, and a woman named 'Umm ul-Musayyib, it tells the story of the Prophet's visit to her home when she was experiencing strong fever. The fever was so extreme that she was shaking. The Prophet, peace and blessings be upon him, asked the woman, "Why are you shaking?" The woman responded, "It is the fever. May Allah not put any blessings in it." The Prophet then continued, and said, "Do not curse the fever, for verily the fever relinquishes the sins as the blacksmith, and the heat from the forge of the blacksmith, relinquishes and takes away the impurities of the iron." From the tale, we learn that the Prophet, peace and blessings be upon him, is a person who is positive towards the situation and towards the *qadr* of Allah, glorified and exalted is He, who allowed the woman to fall ill. As travellers of the journey to the Messenger, peace and blessings be upon him, we ought to try and practice the same attitude towards illnesses within ourselves. Should we visit those who are sick, we should pray, "*Inshaa Allah*, this is a means of purification for you." It is essential that we remain positive internally as well, in order to gain the means of purification of the heart.

> "Take what is given freely, enjoin what is good, and turn away from the ignorant." *Al-A'raf* (7:199),
>
> Ibn ul-Qayyim Al-Jawziyyah, *Ar-Risalat ut-Tabukiyyah*

Fellow scholars have mentioned the beautiful verse

above, and regards it as the comprehensive verse of manners. Here, Allah, glorified and exalted is He, tells us to do three things. First, Allah tells us to take the pardoning that is given freely. For example, a person had cursed his brother's illness. The person then recognises the expression as something bad that he has done, then seeks pardon and looks on the positive side of life. The Prophet, peace and blessings be upon him, said, "I love the person who is optimistic." More often than not, we are presented with a choice to decide the direction in which we wish the situation would take. Always take the direction of being a person who pardons others. With regards to this, a scholar had once mentioned a profound statement, "If you were to deal with people, and expected them to treat you a certain manner all the time, you will never arrive at the expectation that you had hoped for." We should always meet people at the level that they feel safe and comfortable with to express their thoughts and emotions, even when it is difficult for you to hear and accept from your end. A person giving advice ought to maintain his integrity of the *shariah*; however, compassion is just as essential to ensure that you facilitate the situation with kindness. This distinguishes a person who offers advice with manners, and a person who offers without it.

Second, Allah, glorified and exalted is He, tells us to call to good. There shall be instances where people will defy us.

For example, a family member who we cherish may claim that we are too rigid with our principles, and he or she may end up disliking us. However, it is our duty to avoid creating a far greater gap by repelling with the same energy. Become a person who is better in character. In situations as such, silence is the best rebuttal.

> "If you abide by these (three) qualities, whatever the people inflict on you will be good, even if it appears evil — only good can result from enjoining good even if it is encased in a situation of evil and harm." Ibn ul-Qayyim Al-Jawziyyah, *Ar-Risalat ut-Tabukiyyah*

The excerpt above presents the *fiqh* of Ibn Qayyim, may Allah have mercy on him. Although people may intend to create discomfort in us with the speech or actions they wish to deliver or portray, it shall become goodness for us when we utilise the tools that Ibn Qayyim has elaborated as our lens.

> "Allah says, 'Indeed, those who came with falsehood are a group among you. Do not think it is bad for you; rather it is good for you.'"
>
> *An-Nur* (24:11)

Ibn Qayyim, may Allah have mercy on him, then brings forth this verse. He urges us to treat people kindly despite their treatment towards us, and despite their negative treatment towards us, it still remains a good thing for us.

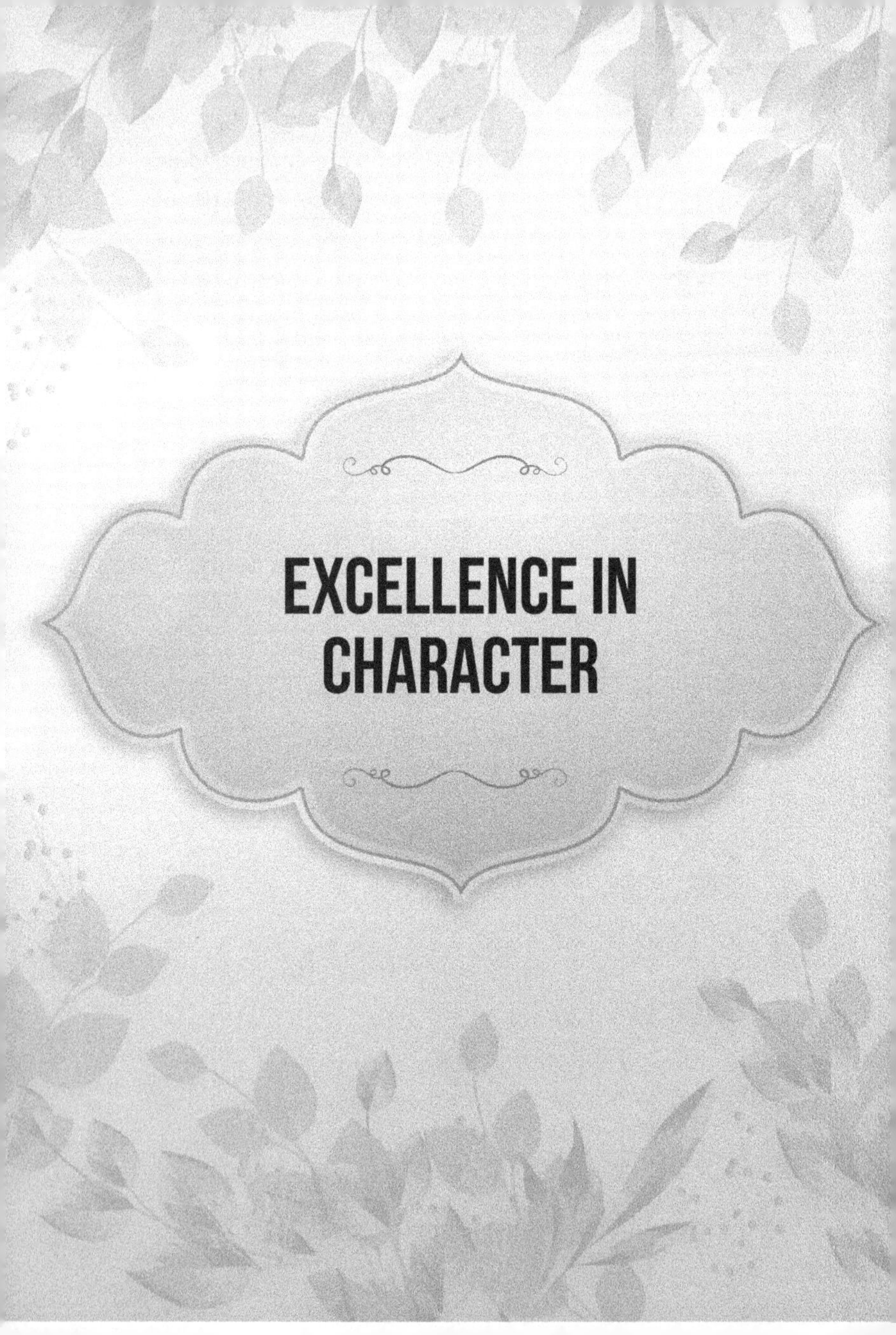

EXCELLENCE IN CHARACTER

A person is unable to attain excellent character without the following three conditions:

1. He must possess good nature that can help him pursue his excellence through knowledge, determination, and action. A rough and dry nature would make it hard for him to submit to this, whereas a mild and smooth nature increases his possibility to receive the plowing and the seeds.
2. He must possess a strong soul capable of conquering calls of laziness, transgression, and desire, all of which contradicts perfection. The souls that cannot defeat this will always be defeated and conquered.
3. He must possess a discerning knowledge of the truth of matters, which would enable him to put things in their rightful position, and to distinguish between flesh and cancer, beads and gems. Ibn ul-Qayyim Al-Jawziyyah, *Ar-Risalat ut-Tabukiyyah*

NOTES

www.ingramcontent.com/pod-product-compliance
Ingram Content Group UK Ltd.
Pitfield, Milton Keynes, MK11 3LW, UK
UKHW021933190726
13853UKWH00004B/1407